David **Willetts** is Member of Parliament for Havant and
Shadow Employment Spokesman. He has served as a Treasury official,
as a member of Margaret Thatcher's Policy Unit and
as Paymaster General in the Cabinet Office.
He has written widely on economic and social issues. His publications
for the Social Market Federation include *The Age of Entitlement*,
Civic Conservatism, and *Is Conservatism Dead?* (with John Gray).
He sits on the SMF's Advisory Council.

Welfare to Work

DAVID WILLETTS

The Social Market Foundation
April 1998

First published by The Social Market Foundation, 1998
in association with Profile Books Ltd

The Social Market Foundation
11 Tufton Street
London SW1P 3QB

Profile Books Ltd
62 Queen Anne Street
London W1M 9LA

Printed in Great Britain by Watkiss Studios Ltd

A CIP catalogue record for this book is available from the British Library.

Paper No. 36

ISBN 1 874097 18 6

Contents

Acknowledgements

I am grateful to Lewis Baston, Joanna Brown, and Jane Dyson
of the House of Commons Library, for their assistance in
the preparation of this pamphlet.
My thanks also to Helga Wright for her unstinting dedication.
I am most grateful to Roderick Nye and Daniel Finkelstein
for their very helpful comments on an earlier draft of this paper.
David Willetts, April 1998

List of Tables

Foreword

Employability matters. Access to the labour market offers the prospect of economic mobility and personal security. Above all, a job is a passport to social inclusion, a gateway to the sorts of choices and sets of responsibilities which those in the mainstream of society take for granted. Can public policy increase employability among those who have become divorced from this mainstream or who were never a part of it to begin with?

This question has been asked by successive governments, both here and abroad, ever since the era of full employment came to an end more than twenty years ago. In that time any number of solutions have been tried and a welter of academic literature has been published on the best way to move people off welfare and into work.

In Britain we are about to embark on the New Deal, perhaps the most ambitious programme ever devised to reintegrate the unemployed into the world of work. Yet, as David Willetts points out, it is more than just a welfare to work scheme writ large.

The New Deal is central to a systematic attempt at social and economic transformation. One which will close the gap between the poor and the rest of society; raise the rate of economic growth by increasing skills levels; redirect public money away from spending on social failure to investing in education and health; and help end social exclusion.

Using data available from other countries and the experience of Britain's own previous schemes, Willetts examines whether the New Deal can achieve everything which is being asked of it. In the process he unravels the myths from the facts about the composition of UK unemployment, the value of training and the difference that welfare to work programmes can actually make.

What emerges is a comprehensive and thoughtful analysis of the factors affecting access to the labour market and the role governments can play in extending it.

Roderick Nye
April 1998

1: Why Welfare to Work Matters

If you were to have a competition for the statistic most frequently used by the government since coming to office last year it would probably be won by:

> Almost one in five households in Britain have no-one in work.
>
> (Tony Blair, *Hansard*, 14 May 1997, col 65)

The message is clear – worklessness is at the heart of Britain's social problems. It is the most vivid evidence offered of the failure of the welfare state as currently constituted. The answer is very simple and stark – work. Gordon Brown in particular speaks about 'encouraging work, encouraging people to work harder, rewarding the work ethic' (*On the Record*, 23 March 1997). His words are echoed by the DSS. 'Work is the best route out of poverty for people who are able to do so' (*The Case for Welfare Reform*, DSS 1998), although the reference to 'those who are able to do so' begs important questions.

Getting people off welfare and into work is the central objective of this government's economic and social policies. Nobody could quarrel with such an obvious and uncontroversial objective. But it also has a particular political significance for a Labour government determined to resolve the dilemmas which brought down its predecessors and anxious to construct a new, progressive political project. The attempt to get people off welfare and into work underpins four crucial and distinctive New Labour propositions.

3

Saving to spend

First, it appears to resolve the public expenditure dilemmas which have troubled previous Labour governments. Gordon Brown claims that the old days of high spending are gone, but at the same time he needs to be able to offer higher spending on particular programmes such as education and health. He has to demonstrate offsetting savings in order to put more into these popular programmes. Hence the claim that too much is being spent on social security to meet 'the costs of failure'. 'We will increase the share of national income spent on education as we decrease it on the bills of economic and social failure' (Tony Blair, Labour Manifesto launch, 3 April 1997).

The key to achieving these savings lies, paradoxically, in spending £5.2 billion of windfall tax proceeds on their welfare to work programme (over £3 billion on the New Deal for the young and the long-term unemployed). The theory is that, despite these costs, they will eventually save money overall on the costs of welfare dependency. The savings released can then be put into other programmes, particularly education. In this way the government can say that it is being fiscally responsible while offering to spend more money on its favourite programmes at the same time. The commitment to Welfare to Work is crucial to making that claim credible.

Training for growth

'Post neo-classical endogenous growth theory' sounds rather pretentious but it does mean something. It is the second way in which welfare to work helps to resolve an Old Labour problem. The claim is that we can raise the growth rate by our own efforts – endogenously – rather than just allowing it to be determined exogenously by factors such as the rate of technological change. In this respect Gordon Brown is very much like Nigel Lawson. Both have wanted to put macro-economic policy on automatic pilot (with a fixed exchange rate rule or an independent bank) so that they could then turn their attention to an ambitious domestic policy agenda to strengthen the supply-side of the economy and thus raise the growth rate. But there the similarities end. For Nigel Lawson and Margaret Thatcher that supply-side agenda was free-market reform (the neo-classical bit of the Gordon Brown quotation). But Gordon Brown is post neo-classical and believes that there is a more active role for government. In the old days that would have meant a Wilsonian national plan if not worse. But Gordon Brown believes that he has found a different way of raising the growth rate, a third way between Lawsonian free-market economics and old-fashioned corporatist planning. If government can raise the skills of the workforce then it will be able to soften the impact of those skills shortages which are supposed to bring every British economic recovery to an unhappy end.

> The modern view is that what causes inflation and what causes unemployment is exactly the same thing . . . the lack of capacity in your economy. So, without an investment-based recovery, every time you grow you get both inflationary pressures and high unemployment. Now we want to tackle unemployment from the supply side, by the measures that will get the young and the

long-term unemployed into effective work through having skills. (Gordon Brown, BBC Debate for a Chancellor, 6 April 1997)

Richard Layard is the most prominent British exponent of this line of argument. He says that we have ended up with a reserve army of the unemployed who do not even carry out the function which the harshest Marxist critic of capitalism expected of them, which was to hold down the wages of those in work by threatening to replace them with new recruits drawn from the ranks of the unemployed. The argument is that the long-term unemployed are so totally excluded from the labour market that they do not even exert downward pressure on wages. They are not reservists, they are non-combatants. So you can raise the growth rate of the economy by reintegrating them into the labour market. Then the economy should be able to enjoy a low rate of inflation combined with a low rate of unemployment.

Redistribution without taxation
This focus on skills is not just a new sort of economic strategy, it is supposed to be a social strategy because it offers a fresh answer to the old question of the distribution of income. It is not true, as Labour claim, that poverty has increased in Britain over the past ten or twenty years. It is true, however, that the income gap widened, at least up until 1993. Peter Lilley and Gordon Brown offer a very similar explanation of this widening of income differentials. They argue that in the modern global economy there has been an increase in returns to cognitive skills relative to unskilled

work. This change has affected all the open Western economies, but responses from national governments have differed. On the continent they have tended to intervene to hold up wages at the bottom of the scale, thus compressing income differentials but at the cost of high rates of unemployment for unskilled people. Alternatively there is the British and American response – a flexible labour market which absorbs many more people into work, albeit sometimes low-paid work, where their wages are then topped up with an Earned Income Tax Credit or a Family Credit or, in future, the Working Families' Tax Credit.

One would expect any Labour government – Old or New – to deplore this widening of income differentials. But what is to be done about it? Previous Labour governments used the tax and benefit system to redistribute income with higher taxes paying higher benefits, together with trade union action to hold up wages. But times have changed. The new government wants to raise the skills of the unemployed or low-paid workers in order to make them employable at a good wage. That way it can narrow the income gap without having to act more directly to redistribute incomes via the tax and benefit system.

Our anti-poverty strategy for this county, starts from the importance of providing opportunities for work. Its founding principle is that we must tackle the causes of poverty, not simply deal with its consequences. It is built around a New Deal programme that offers new opportunities directly to young people.
(Gordon Brown, Centrepoint, 3 December 1997)

So greater equality is going to be achieved by increasing the skills of the less well-off so that they can command better wages, not by scaring the middle-classes with higher taxation.

Including the excluded

In the 1970s Keith Joseph worried about what he called the 'cycle of deprivation'. In the 1980s Charles Murray identified an 'underclass'. Since it was elected, the new government has talked a great deal about social exclusion. Whatever expression one uses, there are clearly a range of deep-seated social problems which go beyond poverty or a widening income distribution and these have resulted in sections of the population, often geographically concentrated, being cut adrift from the expectations and choices which mainstream society takes for granted. With Welfare to Work, Labour claims to have a new policy to address this problem, one which is bolder and more radical than anything which has been tried before.

> Already the new Labour government has put in place the most radical policies for a generation to tackle poverty and social exclusion. That is a big claim but I believe it is justified. The biggest ever programme to get the young and long-term unemployed back to work . . . and soon Britain's first ever statutory minimum wage.
> (Tony Blair, *Independent*, 8 December 1997)

More than a work programme

So we see why so much is riding on the success of welfare to work. For a Labour government it appears to offer four solutions to problems which have bedevilled its predecessors by:

- releasing more public spending for education and other popular programmes within tight overall expenditure control
- raising the growth rate of the economy through increasing the skills of the workforce and reintegrating the long-term unemployed into the jobs market
- reducing income inequality without heavy-handed use of the tax and benefit system to redistribute income
- offering a distinctive and effective solution to the problem of social exclusion.

Welfare to work is not an issue just for the unemployed, its success is central to constructing a modern progressive project for the new government.

There is just one snag. The claims set out above may be bold and imaginative but that does not necessarily make them true. They can all be tested against a large body of evidence gleaned from similar schemes which have been attempted previously in Britain and elsewhere in the world. After analysing Britain's employment problem in the next chapter and briefly describing the New Deal programme in Chapter 3, the book will then investigate these four specific claims in Chapters 4–7.

2: Working People: Workless Households

Here are two statements:

- nearly 20 per cent of working age households in Great Britain are workless, one of the worst rates in the Western world

- OECD figures show that about 70 per cent of the working age population in Great Britain are in work, one of the highest rates in the Western world.

Both statements are true. How can this be? Do we have a problem of worklessness or not? Perhaps a thought-experiment might help explain the puzzle.

Imagine a society where two-thirds of adults are in paid work and one-third are not – because for example they are unemployed or disabled or have domestic responsibilities. Imagine that this is a society of big communitarian families so that each household contains three adults of working age. And finally assume that working and non-working adults are evenly distributed across these households so that each has two workers and one non-working adult. This is a society with no workless households.

Then imagine that this society has an explosion of individualism. All those extended families break up and everyone lives on their own. There is no change in patterns of work. But now this is a society with one-third of households workless. The smaller the average household the greater the risk that a non-worker makes a workless household.

The thought-experiment might be rather schematic but it

Table A
Labour market activity and workless households 1994

	Employment as a percentage of the working age population	Workless households as a percentage of all households
	ratio	households
Spain	47.0	20.1
Italy	51.7	17.2
France	58.7	16.5
Germany	65.4	15.5
UK	69.9	18.9
USA	74.2	11.5

Sources:'It takes two: Employment Polarisation in the OECD'
CEPR Discussion Paper No. 304 (Gregg/Wadsworth)
OECD Employment Outlook, 1997

contains one very important message. The significant
element is changes in the composition of households, not
changes in the job market. Tony Blair's favourite statistic
appears to tell us something important about British jobs but
actually it is telling us something about British families. No
independent observer would think that Britain's rate of
employment was a serious problem – indeed it looks rather
good by international standards. But they would be struck by
the high rate of family break-up, the small average size of
households, and therefore the high propensity to workless
households. The figures above confirm the story.

The table shows that Britain has a higher proportion of its
adults in work than any other advanced European country,
and is surpassed only by America. Yet our percentage rate of
workless households is also one of the worst in the western

world, surpassed in the table only by Spain which has a far lower rate of employment. Any other country which had 70 per cent of its adults in employment would have much less than 19 per cent of its households workless.

How have we ensured that so many British adults are in work? We have not been propping up traditional industries but instead we have moved fast into new industries and services. Often the new jobs have been filled by young people and women. The traditional male manual worker, even if skilled, has been left behind. The glue of financial dependence on a *paterfamilias* earning a 'family wage' disappears as instead young people leave home and make their own way in the world relatively early. Women who find work are less dependent on their partners: Britain has high rates for divorce and of female participation in work. Our large-scale public housing and the rules for allocating it also encourage people to set up new households of their own.

Other western societies have gone a different route. They have tried to protect the traditional jobs of the *paterfamilias*. He has much greater job protection and is difficult to sack. There are few properly-funded pensions schemes so the employer cannot offer him early retirement as soon as he decently can. But their more highly-regulated economies have fewer opportunities for new businesses or for young people and women to move into the jobs of the future. There are some jobs for women but very much as a second division of peripheral workers on temporary contracts – they can be laid off easily if business turns down, unlike the men in the core jobs. (In Britain male unemployment is higher than female: on the continent it tends to be the other

Table B
Unemployment and workless households, Great Britain

	Unemployed claimants ('ooos)	Workless households (%)
1979	1,295.7	8
1988	2,370.4	16
1997	1,614.0	18.5

Source: House of Commons Library & HM Treasury
NB There is a discontinuity in the figures for workless households between 1988 and 1996 because of a shift from using Households Below Average Incomes statistics to the Labour Force Survey. It does not significantly affect the results.

way round.) The traditional family is much stronger: the young and the women rely on the distribution of the man's family wage within the household to maintain their living standards. Such an economy may well have fewer jobs, larger families, and fewer workless households.

The statistics on workless households tell a story of different societies, different cultures, and different patterns of work. It is a rich and interesting story but it is seriously misleading to present it as simply showing that Britain has a problem of worklessness. The government appears to be saying something significant about unemployment but actually it is saying something significant about household change. Table B above shows how little correlation there is between the two.

As unemployment rose in the early 1980s the percentage of workless households increased as well. But even though unemployment then fell and rose again the number of workless households carried on rising steadily, reaching a

Table C
Workless households of working age, Great Britain

	1984	1996	Change 1984-96
All Households			
One adult, children under 16	556	1,267	128%
One adult, no children	1,725	3,253	89%
Two adults, children under 16	4,681	4,729	1%
Two adults, no children	4,509	5,283	17%
Three or more adults, children under 16	1,576	1,214	-23%
Three or more adults, no children	2,717	2,608	-4%
Total	15,764	18,354	16%
Workless Households			
One adult, children under 16	328	787	140%
One adult, no children	581	1,073	85%
Two adults, children under 16	530	501	-5%
Two adults, no children	783	930	19%
Three or more adults, children under 16	101	72	-29%
Three or more adults, no children	177	215	21%
Total	2,500	3,578	43%
Workless Households			
One adult, children under 16	13%	22%	
One adult, no children	23%	30%	
Two adults, children under 16	21%	14%	
Two adults, no children	31%	26%	
Three or more adults, children under 16	4%	2%	
Three or more adults, no children	7%	6%	
Total	100%	100%	

Source: Office of National Statistics. Labour Market Trends, September 1997

17

peak in 1996 before falling back in 1997. It shows how little changes in unemployment explain changes in the number of workless households.

The table on the previous page tries a different approach. We begin by breaking down households into different groups to get a clear picture of household change between 1984 and 1996. There have been big increases in the number of small households – either a lone childless adult or a lone parent. These are types of household with quite a high propensity to worklessness. Households of two adults with children (the image of a workless household which still springs to mind) are 14 per cent of workless households and their absolute numbers are declining. More than half of workless households have only one adult.

The rise in the number of workless households is thus largely driven by the increase in the number of households with a tendency to be workless.

We are sometimes told (for example by Paul Gregg, one of the government's special advisers) that we are becoming two nations – of work-rich and of work-poor households. There are several mutually consistent explanations of this. Like tends to marry like, so people with the background and skills which give them a good chance in the labour market tend to marry each other and similarly the less employable tend to marry each other (known as assortative mating). If one partner loses his or her job the other may stop working so that they can enjoy their enforced leisure together (known as the co-consumption effect). But equally the benefits system itself may be a culprit because Income Support focuses on household income. If a man loses his job his working wife's modest earnings may mean that they have no entitlement to Income Support which in turn would offer help with the mortgage and passports to various other forms of assistance. Their income might be higher if she was not working at all. This is a real problem. The radical solution is for the benefits system always to deal with individuals – as the tax system now does – rather than households. As so much of the rest of life becomes more individualistic the pressure will rise for social security to go the same way. But it is a very expensive option indeed. It also cuts across our instinctive belief that man and wife have an obligation to look after each other before turning to the state for help. This issue however – measuring the income of the individual or the household – generates enormous confusion in discussions of social policy.

Gordon Brown wants to focus the responsibility on individuals rather than the family for distributing income among its members. This may help explain why he seems to expect every individual to be working.

Compare the following two propositions:

We are . . . introducing the minimum wage, which will help those on low income.
(Tony Blair, *Hansard*, 11 June 1997, col 1140)

As protests by disabled campaigners reached the gates of Downing Street yesterday, the government claimed that £10 billion a year in disabilities benefits is paid to better-off households.
(*Daily Mail*, 23 December 1997)

The first proposition focuses on the effect of the minimum wage on individuals. But if instead you look at the impact of the minimum wage on households the position is rather different. The Institute for Fiscal Studies has shown that many people earning low pay are actually in quite affluent households. For this reason the richest third of households actually gain more from the minimum wage than the poorest third of households.

Disability benefits are payable to an individual to compensate for a disability. Some people who receive them are indeed in affluent households.

You cannot have it both ways and look at individuals in one case in order to support the arguments for the minimum wage and then look at households in another case in order to support a different policy on disability benefits.

3: The Welfare to Work Programme

The windfall levy on the utilities will raise a total of £5.2 billion. The breakdown of expenditure on the government's New Deal for the young and the long-term unemployed is set out in Table D below. The balance goes on a schools capital programme (£1.3 billion), and further measures for groups such as lone parents.

It is perhaps significant that the profile of expenditure shown in the table below does not suggest that the scheme's costs will gradually fall so that it becomes self-financing. Instead welfare to work is estimated to cost slightly more in 2001-02 than in 1998-99.

The bulk of the expenditure is on young unemployed people, although as Table E shows there are actually more people aged over 25 unemployed for more than two years.

Gordon Brown announced his programme to help the 250,000 young people who had been unemployed for six

Table D
Financing Welfare to Work

	£ million					
	1997-98	1998-99	1999-00	2000-01	2001-02	**1997-02**
Spending on the programme:						
A New Deal for young people	100	580	650	640	640	**2,610**
A New Deal for the long-term unemployed	0	120	160	90	80	**450**
Sub-total	**100**	**700**	**810**	**730**	**720**	**3,060 ***

Source: Table 3.1, HM Treasury Red Book, March 1998.

* Constituent items may not sum because of rounding.

Table E
Unemployed claimants by age and duration in the UK

	Number of claimants	Aged 18-24 unemployed	Aged 25+ unemployed
	total	over 6 months	over 2 years
October 1995	2,212,000	249,000	424,000
January 1998 (latest month)	1,479,000	118,000	216,000
Change:			
October 1995 – January 1998	-733,000	-131,000	-208,000
	(-33.1%)	(-52.6%)	(-49.1%)

Source: ONS

months or more back in October 1995. Since that time the number of 18–24 year olds in that category has more than halved. Indeed the two categories of unemployed people covered by the New Deal have fallen more rapidly than unemployment in total. Table E also shows that there are nearly twice as many long-term unemployed as young unemployed. Yet the pattern of spending is heavily biased towards the smaller group. There is as yet no clear statement of how the money in the New Deal for young unemployed people will be spent, even in 1998-99. The table below is assembled drawing on information from Parliamentary Answers and rather fuller figures given by the Scottish Office to the Scottish Select Committee (Scottish Affairs Committee, *Welfare to Work in Scotland: the New Deal*, House of Commons Paper 335, volume II, pp. 138-9).

Table F
Expenditure on the New Deal for the young unemployed
1998–99

Stock of unemployed claimants aged 18–24 and out of work for over six months, April 1998			100,000
Flow per month into six-month duration threshold			14,000
Total client group during year (April 1998 stock plus 12 * monthly flow)			268,000

	participants number	cost per participant (£)	total cost (£million)
Gateway cost (£260 per participant; all participants)		260	70
40% of participants (112,000) are expected to leave directly from the Gateway, leaving 168,000 to participate in the New Deal options, broken down as follows:	160,800		
40% in subsidised work with a £60 top-up for an average of 22 weeks, plus a one-off contribution of £750 to training.	64,320	2,070	133
25% in education and training at a cost of £2,300 for 39 weeks plus a £43 per week training allowance	40,200	3,977	160
25% on the environmental task force at a cost of £2,750 for 20 weeks plus a £43 per week allowance	40,200	3,910	157
10% on voluntary work for an averageof 20 weeks	16,080	3,910	63
Total cost			**583**

4: Will It Save Money?

We will reduce spending on the costs of unemployment
and increase it on education.
(Tony Blair, Press Release, 8 February 1997)

Active labour market policies are not new. Many countries
have been tempted by the idea of putting public money into
making the unemployed more employable. They too have
hoped to save money in the long term, to raise the skills of
the workforce, and thus their growth rate, and to increase the
incomes and opportunities of the disadvantaged.

Gordon Brown likes to give the impression that no
British government has tried to do this in the past and that
the unemployed have simply been left to collect their benefit
cheques. The last Conservative government actually tried a
variety of schemes and many have been independently
evaluated by bodies such as the Policy Studies Institute.

Similar schemes have also been tried in Sweden, in
Australia, and in many parts of the USA. In fact, just about
every combination of training, education, tax incentives and
work requirements has been implemented in at least one
advanced Western country over the past ten or fifteen years.
A distinguished expert on the subject, when presented with
an apparently novel suggestion at a seminar observed, 'They
tried that in Finland in 1987'. It ought to be every policy
wonk's epitaph.

The Organisation of Economic Co-operation and
Development (OECD) has brought together the international
evidence on what works and what doesn't. By and large the
results from the appraisals of these schemes make dispiriting
reading. Many schemes achieve little. Only a very few

achieve much. None has been able to deliver all the objectives which the government has set itself. Why then is it so difficult in practice to do what looks so plausible in theory?

Deadweight costs

The biggest problem is deadweight costs – money spent putting people on schemes who are likely to have secured a job by their own efforts. The best way to measure the deadweight problem is to set up a control group of non-participants who resemble as closely as possible those participating in the scheme. One can then compare outcomes between the two groups.

The greatest variety of schemes which have been appraised most rigorously are to be found in the United States of America. One of the very best, which has been brought to international attention, is GAIN (Greater Avenues to Independence) in Riverside County, California. It often appears in media reports as a model of what welfare to work schemes can achieve. But the hard-headed appraisals of the scheme show that the best GAIN managed to achieve for quite high expenditure was a 9 per cent higher rate of work by participants than non-participants. Moreover, there is a half-life effect with the benefits of the scheme tending to wear off on those who have been through it over time. By year three only 5 per cent fewer participants on the scheme were dependent on America's means-tested benefit, then called AFDC (Aid for Families with Dependent Children) than was the case with the control group of non-participants. Many schemes do far worse than this.

In order to save money on overall benefit expenditure (and to reap extra money in tax revenues) it is absolutely essential to hold deadweight costs to a minimum. It is not good enough just to show that people participating in the scheme get jobs. If they would have moved off benefits and into tax paying jobs anyway, then there is no favourable impact on the exchequer from the scheme. That impact depends on showing that something extra has been achieved over and above what would have happened anyway, which more than offsets the cost of the extra expenditure.

How might you set about designing a scheme which held deadweight costs to a minimum? There are two obvious ways of doing it which we will look at in turn – firstly, focusing on measures which massively transform people's job prospects and secondly, focusing on people who would otherwise have had a very low chance of finding work.

The evidence from abroad and also from previous experience in Britain is that job subsidies are particularly ineffective at improving people's chances of getting a job. In Britain from 1986 to 1990 the then government offered a subsidy to long-term unemployed claimants who had to accept a full-time job paying less than £90 per week after which they would then qualify for a subsidy. An independent evaluation reported a deadweight effect of 69 per cent.

As always, one can find rigorously evaluated experiments in America. Some of them even suggest there is a perverse effect from identifying individuals as requiring a subsidy:

In 1981 a Dayton, Ohio, manpower agency randomly divided able-bodied welfare recipients into three groups.

Each member of the first group was given a tax credit
voucher informing prospective employers that the
applicant was eligible for the Targeted Jobs Tax Credit
and outlining the precise nature of the credit. Members
of the second group were given comparable wage
subsidy vouchers that provided reimbursement through a
cash payment rather than a tax credit. The purpose of this
was to test whether the low response rate was created by
a fear of a possible tax audit associated with the credit. All
participants were encouraged to show the vouchers
when they applied for jobs. The third group was not
given any voucher.

In a recent analysis of the Dayton experiment, Burtless
found that 21 per cent of the unvouchered group found
jobs within an eight-week job search period, but only 13
per cent of the vouchered groups found jobs. No
significant differences between the two types of vouchers
were found. Of the vouchered job finders, only one-
quarter of their employers bothered to apply for the
subsidy. This suggests that tax credit schemes may identify
and stigmatise job applicants as being from a
disadvantaged group.

(Bassi and Ashenfelter, 'Direct Job Creation and Training Programmes', in
Fighting Poverty, ed Sheldon H Danziger and Daniel H Weinberg, p145)

The general evidence from Britain and abroad is that job
subsidies are a particularly expensive way of helping
unemployed people. They cost a lot of money and do not
appear to yield results which are much better than the
absence of such schemes altogether.

Table G
Probability of those on benefit in April 1996 being off benefit by April 1997

Age:	18–24	25+
All	84%	69%
Unemployed over 6 months in April 1996	80%	60%
Unemployed over 2 years in April 1996	n/a	44%

Source: House of Commons Library and NERA evidence to Education & Employment Committee, HC 263-11

You might however be able to do rather better with such schemes if you focused them very precisely on particular disadvantaged groups with a very high risk of remaining unemployed. This is certainly one of the main conclusions to emerge from OECD studies for such schemes. They favour narrowly targeted programmes which, they argue, are much more cost-effective than large-scale national schemes. But this is not advice which our government has followed in designing their welfare to work scheme. Here are the figures showing the chances of different groups unemployed people of getting off benefit.

Table G above gives figures on the probability of leaving benefit within the coming year. The table shows that a young person unemployed for more than six months in April 1996 had an 8 in 10 chance of being off benefit 12 months later. We can show the same phenomenon on a monthly basis. Some 18 per cent of young unemployed people leave the register every month, as against 13 per cent of claimants aged over 25. Among 18–24 year olds who have been unemployed for more than six months, 12 per cent leave the register every month as against 8.5 per cent for people aged over 25 and unemployed for more than six months.

The evidence is absolutely clear: young people have the best chance of getting off benefit. This is not surprising. Young people are trying out different ways of work and different ways of living. They move on and off benefit as they try out different jobs and reject employers or careers which do not suit them (most people leaving employment do so voluntarily rather than as a result of being made redundant and this is particularly true of young people). Young people are searching more intensively than ever to find the right job and moving on and off benefit as they do so. People aged under 30 account for 60 per cent of new job engagements. So it is seriously misleading to imagine that young people are the ones who are likely to get stuck unemployed for a long period of time. They are likely to experience spells of unemployment, but it is older people who are much more likely to get stuck unemployed if they do lose their jobs.

The number of young people unemployed for more than six months is also falling fast – indeed, faster than total unemployment.

Yet of the £3.1 billion welfare to work budget over 80 per cent, or £2.6 billion, is going to young people unemployed for more than six months. Less than 20 per cent of the budget, £450 million, is going to the 200,000 people who have been unemployed for more than two years. And there is little extra help for anyone other than the young person who has been unemployed for up to two years. So a

47-year-old man who has not worked for 18 months gets
little assistance under welfare to work whereas a 21-year-old
unemployed for only one-third of the time will get access to
an extremely expensive programme. The Budget announced
some concessions but the discrimination against the older
unemployed is stark. Indeed, this may be one of the reasons
for the government's decision not to ban age discrimination
in recruitment advertisements. Andrew Smith, the
Employment Minister, explained in the debate on the
subject in the House of Commons on 6 February 1998 that
'the New Deal would therefore be caught by the Bill' (col
1416). The tail really does seem to be wagging the dog if the
government cannot fulfil its pledge to legislate on age
discrimination because its own New Deal discriminates by
age.

One explanation which is offered in defence of this bias is
the claim that although young people may be less at risk of
getting stuck long-term unemployed, if they do then get
stuck in such a situation then a whole life can be wasted. But
the evidence is that they are much less likely to get stuck
even after six months of unemployment than older age
groups. This is perhaps because they have much greater
flexibility and capacity for change and renewal. The people
who risk getting stuck are older workers who have
developed a particular skill or expertise which has suddenly
been devalued as a result of technological or industrial
change.

There is a second, less charitable explanation of the age
bias in the scheme. By choosing a group which already has
the highest chance of moving off benefit, the government

may claim the credit for what would have happened anyway. The only problem with hitting a target which would have been hit anyway is that this is not going to save any money at all.

This criticism is well understood by the government, which counters with the fact that youth unemployment is still higher than for other age groups:

> I want the target to be to reduce unemployment among people under 25 to the same level as that among adult workers – rather than it being double or treble that level. (David Blunkett, House of Commons, 26 June 1997, cols 973-974).

It is true that Britain's headline rate of unemployment among under-25s is higher than the rate of unemployment among older people. But this on its own does not guarantee that the programme is well-targeted with low deadweight costs and therefore is likely to yield overall exchequer savings. As we saw, a lot of this unemployment is frictional unemployment, young people experimenting with a variety of jobs and moving on and off benefit as they move between jobs. If we compare Britain's position with other advanced western countries we see that we actually do rather well on youth employment but our particular problem is older men who are trapped in long-term unemployment. A recent report from the TUC makes the point very well. It cites the latest European Commission estimates which show UK youth unemployment at 13.1 per cent, significantly lower than the EU average of 20.3 per cent. However, the UK had a higher share of its unemployed made up of older men over 25 who have been out of work for more than two years (38 per cent), as against an EU average of 32 per cent.

Any neutral international observer looking at the British labour market would not think that our problem was youth unemployment but the waste of skill and experience among older male workers. These people are much more likely to be stuck long-term on benefit, and therefore represent a far greater potential saving for the exchequer.

Substitution

Imagine that you have solved the problem of deadweight and you have succeeded in placing in jobs young unemployed people who would not otherwise have got them. That isn't the end of the story. The next problem you face is substitution. Imagine that you are a big firm recruiting say 1,000 young people a year. You sign up to the New Deal and get good publicity for it. You go out and recruit some people through the New Deal. These will either be people you would have recruited anyway (deadweight) or else they will displace others who would have been recruited instead (substitution). There is no suggestion that these firms will be recruiting more people in total.

There is nothing in the government's programme that will increase the capacity of the British economy to create jobs (indeed the government may actually be doing things in other policy areas which will reduce the number of jobs created). As Peter Robinson of the LSE observed in his evidence to the Employment Select Committee:

'Recruitment subsidies do not create many new jobs' (Education and Employment Sub-Committee Report, House of Commons Paper 263, Vol. II). Those people who find jobs will therefore displace others who would have got them otherwise. The programme simply spreads the experience of unemployment more widely and churns more people through the benefits system.

It is actually one of the purposes of the scheme to substitute one group of employees for another. It is difficult to see, however, how such churning will yield any significant saving on total public expenditure on unemployed people. Meanwhile, it means more job insecurity for people who have already found work.

These schemes look affordable when the economy is in good shape and unemployment is falling. But they cost a lot for each individual participant. When the economy starts to slow down and unemployment rises, the high spending per individual proves unsustainable. At the time they are needed most their expense means that they cannot be continued. The cost of the policy of guaranteeing four options with no fifth option is such that the government has not dared extend the full-blown scheme beyond 18–24 year olds. The full four options are not guaranteed for all long-term unemployed and certainly not for other groups.

Similar schemes have been tried in Scandinavia in particular and have always had to be abandoned when the pressure of rising unemployment makes them unaffordable. The absence of any provision to finance them after the windfall tax runs out suggests that this scheme could prove similarly difficult to sustain.

Conclusion

We have seen that there are three main reasons why the government's welfare to work programme is unlikely to save money:

- such schemes do not significantly increase people's chances of finding work above what they would otherwise have been
- the bulk of the expenditure is focused on young people who are particularly mobile and have particularly good chances of getting off benefits and into work (deadweight)
- as the scheme does not generate more jobs overall, even if it does succeed in placing more unemployed people into work, they will substitute for others who will become unemployed instead (substitution).

Where does this leave the Chancellor? He has claimed unambiguously:

> We will seek to transfer resources from welfare into education and we believe that the plans that we have put forward, including our proposals for dealing with youth and long-term unemployment, will achieve this effect. (Press conference, 10 April 1997).

There will be a temptation to use ingenious definitional changes to disguise the evidence that the scheme is not actually saving much money. Participants in the scheme will not be receiving benefit in the form of the Jobseeker's

Allowance but instead, we are told, they will be receiving 'an allowance equivalent to the value of the benefit'. That means that if they participate on the scheme, social security expenditure on Jobseeker's Allowance is automatically reduced. As spending on the scheme does not count as part of the DSS budget or even part of the overall control total of public expenditure, the Chancellor apparently succeeds in reducing public expenditure at a stroke. Moreover, participants in the welfare to work programme automatically cease to count as unemployed on either the claimant count definition or the labour force survey definition. So you can appear to reduce public expenditure and appear to reduce unemployment even though you are not actually yielding any genuine savings for the exchequer or creating any real new jobs. The trouble with this ingenuity is that it does not produce any extra resources to put into education. If that is still the objective, the government will have to look elsewhere either by directly diverting some of the windfall tax (as has already happened with some education capital expenditure) or by looking to other sources such as the Lottery, or other forms of taxation. Either way, the New Deal will not deliver the shift in the underlying pattern of public expenditure which was supposed to be one of its main aims.

5: Will It Raise the Growth Rate?

> In the global market place, traditional national economic
> policies – corporation from the old Left, isolationist
> ideology from the new Right – no longer have any
> relevance . . . A more educated and adaptable workforce
> is essential for both individual prosperity and economic
> success. That is why the central economic aims of a new
> Labour government will be to increase educational
> opportunity for all and modernise the welfare state.
> (Gordon Brown, 26 February 1997)

We have established that welfare to work is most unlikely to
save money in the short to medium term. But there are
other arguments for the programme irrespective of whether
it redirects public spending. There is the claim that investing
in the skills of the least well-off will raise the growth rate
(and also redistribute incomes, a claim we will investigate in
Chapter 6).

The programme could be expected to raise the skills of
the workforce in several ways. Those deadweight candidates
who would have got jobs anyway will be entitled to one day
a week of employer-provided education and training.
Indeed, one of the reasons why the costs of the New Deal
are so high is that, on top of the £60 per week job subsidy
for the young unemployed, there is also an up-front payment
of £750 to the employer to cover the cost of training as well.
The option of working for the voluntary sector or the
environmental task force is also supposed to raise the
employability of the participants and to have an element of
education and training. Another option is to go into full-
time education and training.

Even if it does not lead directly to net expenditure savings or even a net increase in unemployment, the argument is that the New Deal should over time raise the skills and employability of the workforce and enable the economy to grow faster. As the lack of expenditure savings becomes more apparent this skills argument for welfare to work will increasingly be brought to the fore. But is it any more robust than the previous claim?

The training myth

One of the great platitudes of contemporary politics is that we must do more to train people, but public training schemes are perhaps the most overrated labour market policy we have. This was demonstrated in one famous American experiment in Seattle and Denver in the 1970s. One of the findings from that carefully evaluated programme was that unemployed people offered training fared less well in getting jobs than those without training. Everybody is so used to assuming that training is unambiguously a good thing that this result met with some surprise. But actually the explanation is fairly straightforward.

Imagine that a training scheme increases the wages someone can command by say 50p an hour (actually quite an optimistic assumption). So far, so good. But the people running the schemes are so keen to market it, with a contract to the local TEC and with all the pressure for the New Deal to succeed, that they give the participants very optimistic expectations of what the training can deliver for them in terms of employment. Trainees think therefore that their earning power has gone up by £1 an hour as a result of the scheme. So the gap between their reserve wage (what they think they are worth) and the wage they can actually obtain has widened. In theory training is supposed to narrow that gap and make people more employable. In practice it can end up doing the opposite.

Here we have assumed that training has actually raised people's skills, at least to some extent. But sadly there are doubts about the value of some NVQs and GNVQs. Some carry little or no premium in the labour market – suggesting that employers regard them as worth very little.

The state's real responsibility is not for training but for education. There are some unemployed people whose problems are clear – they are neither numerate nor literate. The state education system has let them down and the New Deal is one way of trying to rectify this failure.

Some further education will also be provided under the New Deal and that too may have its value. The problem here may be a different one. Some courses will include students from modest backgrounds who have lost all their maintenance grants studying alongside those from the New Deal who will be receiving an income equivalent to Jobseeker's Allowance payments and retaining entitlement to any passported benefits. The potential impact of these two, seemingly contradictory, policies will be to create a perverse incentive to get to college via the New Deal after a period of unemployment.

Employers and training

Training is most effective when both employers and

employees can see what they are getting out of it. When talking to people on the shop floor about training, that they tend not to say they are getting NVQ Level 2. Instead they are more likely to say 'they sent me on a course in Germany to learn how to operate the new machine they bought'. That does not show up in the statistics as training but it is no less valuable for that.

The experts designing the New Deal are well aware of the ineffectiveness of some conventional training schemes. They have responded by trying to link employment and training wherever possible. Obviously this cannot apply with the education and training option, but there may be some scope for tying in the practical job experience in the voluntary sector or the environmental sector with a training course. The ideal model for ministers is one in which participants in the New Deal have subsidised work with a private-sector employer and training at the same time. This is a step forward, but it does not necessarily solve the problem.

The implicit assumption is that without the special subsidies in the welfare to work scheme employers would not have been providing any training for their new recruits. But that is far from the case. So there is a deadweight argument on training too. Training would have been provided for many of these young recruits anyway.

The way the public authorities have tried to escape the charge that they are paying employers to do what they would have done in any case is to intervene to require rather different training than is normal company policy. This has already become one of the main sources of employer complaint about the scheme. They find the training requirements of the New Deal cut across their usual training programmes for their new recruits. This is particularly a problem with the larger enterprises that already have well-developed in-house company training schemes. The price of avoiding deadweight might be to require employers to distort their training schemes in ways they think undesirable, and make them more like the conventional public-sector training schemes which tend to do less well.

Rewarding skills vs the minimum wage

There is another paradox here in the government's approach. The stress on skills sits very oddly with the government's arguments on a minimum wage. A minimum wage of £3.50 an hour is forecast to threaten 800,000 job losses if we assume the restoration of half differentials, that is retaining 50% of the gap between rates of pay for skilled and unskilled work. If we assume much lower effects on differentials, we get a lower figure. In order to claim that there will be no significant impact on jobs, the government must also claim that there will be no significant impact on differentials. If that is the case it seems to conflict with the government's stated desire to encourage people to obtain more qualifications, to go out and be trained. The argument they use here is that these people will receive better pay as a reward for staying at college and securing City and Guilds or national vocational qualifications.

Let us suppose an untrained person is working as a kitchen assistant earning £3 an hour, which perhaps goes up to £4 an hour. The person working alongside him, who has a City and Guilds qualification in catering, currently earns

£4 an hour. Will that person accept that there was no point in his obtaining a City and Guilds qualification and that he might as well be untrained? If the government want to encourage people to go out and obtain City and Guilds or national vocational qualifications, they must accept that the person who is currently working for £4 an hour will feel a bit of an idiot if he is working for exactly the same pay as the untrained person alongside him. If the person who is earning £4 an hour and has a qualification is to feel that obtaining that qualification was not a complete waste of time, he or she will expect some increase in pay to compensate.

If you believe in training, you also have to believe in differentials which make such training worthwhile. If you want to believe that the minimum wage will not cost many jobs, you have to argue that differentials at the bottom of the earnings scale will be compressed. But you cannot claim both.

The substitution effect: getting a toe-hold

What about the argument that it is good for the employed to get a toe-hold in the labour market? This is the claim that anything which gets the longer-term unemployed into work, even at the expense of others, is nevertheless worthwhile because it raises the overall level of employability of the workforce.

If you look not at public expenditure costs but at raising the quality of the workforce, the substitution effect we identified in the last chapter suddenly looks rather more desirable. Substitution actually becomes the main point of the programme. This is an interesting argument and its main advocate, Professor Richard Layard, is now a special adviser at the Department for Education and Employment. He argues that people who have lost touch with the world of work are liable to become less and less employable. If they can be got into jobs in place of the more attractive candidates who are more readily employable then we are left with a more employable group of unemployed people. As the economy expands they will find jobs more easily and the economy will be able to operate with a smaller stock of unemployed people overall.

The argument rests on the so-called 'cut flowers' theory or to give it its more pretentious title, 'hysteresis'. The assumption is that once out of work one's skills start depreciating and it is necessary to invest in training to make one more employable.

Richard Layard's theory has, however, been challenged by David Webster of Glasgow Council. He says that instead of focusing on the people who are unemployed we should look instead at the areas where they live and the jobs which are available. What if the long-term unemployed are just like the short-term unemployed but they happen to have been unemployed for rather longer? There may not be a distinct subset of long-term unemployed who are somehow different from the rest. Instead the problem may be that they live in areas of intense unemployment so there are not enough jobs for people to get back into work quickly. If this argument is true, then even if there were valuable training schemes for the unemployed they would not do much to help the long-term unemployed in the absence of economic revival in the depressed areas where they are concentrated. David Webster's is not a full account of the problem but it does remind us that instead of just looking at unemployed people we should also look at the circumstances in which they find out themselves. This is something to which we will return in Chapter 7.

There is a compromise between the Layard and Webster views. There may be particular difficulties facing long-term unemployed people in getting back into work. But these difficulties may not be so much the lack of hard skills and training as psychological barriers. People who have been unemployed for a long time may lose their self-confidence and lack the drive to get themselves back into work. They may become demoralised. And employers may wrongly assume that if someone has been unemployed for a while, there must be something wrong with them, so they will regard taking on such a person as too much of a risk. This suggests that there does need to be extra help so that the long-term unemployed can get back into work. But full-blown training schemes may not really be the answer. Instead what is needed is intense pressure to help them recover their morale and their self-confidence. At the same time we need to reduce what employers see as the riskiness of taking on someone who has been unemployed for quite a while.

The evaluations of the many schemes which the previous government introduced support this view. Job Clubs help unemployed people to write CVs and present themselves properly to employers; they have been shown in some evaluations to be very effective.

The politically neutral Policy Studies Institute recently

looked at Work Trials which involve employers giving three-week trials to people who have been out of work for at least six months (*The Impact of Public Job Placing Programmes*, Michael White, Steve Lissenburgh, and Alex Bryson, Policy Studies Institute, 1997). During the trial the candidates are paid their usual benefit entitlement. At the end of the trial if the unemployed person wants to stay on and the employer wants to take them on, then a normal contract of employment begins. The PSI describes work trials as 'extremely successful'. It increased the chances of employment for both men and women by 35-40 per cent, a far better result than for just about any other programme, including Job Clubs. The author of the study observed that this suggested that the New Deal 'is perhaps an unnecessarily expensive programme' (*Financial Times*, 16 July 1997).

The reason why the New Deal looks so expensive whereas Work Trials and Job Clubs look relatively effective is now becoming clear. The latter do not make any ambitious claims about giving people new skills or transforming their prospects. Instead they just aim to boost their confidence and give the employer a nudge to at least give them a chance. The New Deal will be doing well if, when it is finally evaluated, it is as effective as these programmes which it is replacing.

Conclusion

The model on which the welfare to work programme rests is that you take an unskilled unemployed person, and turn them into a skilled unemployed person or perhaps a skilled person in a subsidised job. Then after the investment in training pays off, they become a skilled employed person. The evidence is increasingly clear, however, that this is not the way the labour market works. Instead a better model is to think of starting with an unskilled unemployed person and help them to become an unskilled employed person. After that the employer and the employee can between them be expected to start investing in raising the employee's skills.

This second approach has several advantages. It goes with the grain of the labour market. It focuses on the particular practical problems which stand in the way of long-term unemployed people getting jobs by simply trying to match them better with employers and reduce the risk for employers of taking them on. It is also a far more cost-effective way of helping the young and the long-term unemployed.

6: Will It Redistribute Income?

A better-trained and educated population not only raises productivity and living standards. It helps reduce inequalities by giving people increased earnings power. (Tony Blair, LIFFE lecture, 16 September 1996)

The analysis in the previous chapter showed that publicly sponsored training schemes were overrated as a means of getting unemployed people into work. That same analysis also suggests that such schemes are unlikely to have a significant impact on income distribution. In this chapter I want to try in a different way to put into perspective the claims that somehow the welfare to work scheme can have a significant impact on income distribution – that it can deliver the same or better results than previous Labour governments have achieved by taxation and benefit policies. This approach draws on work by Professor J Heckman of Chicago University whose paper, 'Is Job Training Oversold?' appeared in *Public Interest*, Spring 1994, pp.91-115. I am most grateful to Lewis Baston for researching the UK data and providing the tables which appear in this chapter.

We will be begin by assuming away all the problems that have been identified so far. We will assume that the £3.5 billion on the New Deal for young people and long-term unemployed is money very well spent. We will assume that all of it, whether it goes directly into training or education or simply job subsidies and working on the environmental task force, yields a significant and useful investment in human capital. We will assume that the investment in human capital yields a 10 per cent rate of return to participants – as good an effect as very good schemes anywhere in the world, even ones focusing much more narrowly on particular target groups. That means that after the four-year term of this £3.5 billion programme, participants in the scheme should be earning a total of £350 million a year more than they otherwise would have been. I doubt if the scheme's most passionate advocate would claim more than that.

Let us now look at how such an effect compares with the pattern of earnings in this country. Since 1979 the incomes of all occupational groups have risen in real terms but the incomes of the less well-qualified or the unqualified have increased by less than the incomes of people with qualifications. Imagine that one wanted to restore income differentials to what they were in 1979. In Table H we get some measure of the scale of the change in income differentials since 1979.

Now we can calculate the size of the increase in incomes which would be necessary restore the same ratios of pay for the unqualified and the better-qualified as obtained in 1979. Table I (page 58) shows how the arithmetic goes. In order to restore 1979 income differentials one has to secure an extra £24 billion per year of income for the less well qualified. Assuming a favourable rate of return of 10 per cent this means an investment in training of £240 billion.

Perhaps it might be helpful to follow the methodology through with one particular example – a man with no qualifications. His income has gone up by 13.8 per cent between 1979 and 1995, whereas for a man with a degree real income has gone up by 33 per cent. To restore the 1979 income differential a man with no qualifications would need to have earnings not of £250 but of £293 per week. That

Table H
Widening income differentials since 1979

Median gross weekly earnings (20 to 69-year-olds)	Degree	Higher Education short of degree	A Level or equivalent	O Level or equivalent	CSE or equivalent	No qualifications
Male						
1979 (in 1979 £s)	135	108	94	96	89	83
1979 (in 1995 £s)	355	284	247	253	234	218
1995 (£)	473	363	318	285	260	250
Change 79/95 (%)	**+33.2**	**+27.8**	**+28.7**	**+12.6**	**+11.1**	**+14.7**
Female						
1979 (in 1979 £s)	96	82	66	58	57	53
1979 (in 1995 £s)	253	216	174	153	150	139
1995 (£)	363	312	229	206	198	167
Change 79/95 (%)	**+43.5**	**+44.4**	**+31.6**	**+34.6**	**+32.0**	**+20.1**

Source: General Household Surveys 1979, 1995
Real 1979 earnings calculated using RPI (Source: Economic Trends 1985, 1997)

Table I
Restoring income differentials to their 1979 levels (£)

	1979 ratio to degree	1995 degree earnings	1995 target earnings	1995 actual earnings	Difference (weekly)	Difference (annual)
Men (no qualifications)	0.62	473	293	250	43	2,408
Men (CSE)	0.66	473	312	260	52	2,704
Women (no qualifications)	0.55	363	200	167	33	1,716
Women (CSE)	0.59	363	214	198	16	832

Source: Lewis Baston

Table J
The size of investment to restore 1979 income differentials

	Investment per person	People affected	Cost
Male (no qualifications)	£24,000	4.5 million	£108.0 billion
Male (CSE)	£27,000	1.5 million	£ 40.5 billion
Female (no qualifications)	£17,000	4.6 million	£ 78.2 billion
Female (CSE)	£8,300	1.6 million	£ 13.3 billion
Total			£240 billion

Source: Lewis Baston

means an extra £2,400 a year. That means an investment in training him of £24,000. There are 4.5 million unqualified men in work so a training investment to raise their incomes would cost £108 billion. The total cost of £240 billion comes simply from including also men with GCSEs and no more and also unqualified women and women with GCSEs and no more.

Of course the figures are schematic, indeed absurd. But the point underlying it is a very serious one. Given the number of people in the British workforce and the size of their incomes it is nonsense to claim that a £3.5 billion welfare to work scheme is going to have any significant impact on the distribution of income nationwide. It is obvious that it would take a scheme many times larger than one currently envisaged to actually close the earnings gap between the qualified and relatively unqualified.

7: Will It Deal With Social Exclusion?

WILL IT DEAL WITH SOCIAL EXCLUSION?

I want all of you to feel part of what I believe is a
national crusade to clear for once and for all the social
divisions that are entrenched in our society because of
unemployment.
(Gordon Brown at the launch of the New Deal pilot,
Tayside Pathfinders, 5 January 1998)

There is one argument left for Welfare to Work. One can
abandon the claims to save money, raise the growth rate, or
have a significant impact on the pattern of income
distribution. Instead one could try a different approach and
target the problem of 'social exclusion'. This is a new phrase
for what Keith Joseph called the 'cycle of deprivation' in the
1970s and Charles Murray called 'the underclass' in the
1980s.

The government is reluctant to define social exclusion
but we all know what it is – that interconnected set of
problems which blight some of our inner cities and also
some estates on the edges of our prosperous conurbations.
The problems are low school performance, high
unemployment, high crime rates, unstable families, large
public housing estates of poor quality, all adding up to high
rates of social deprivation. These also happen to be the areas
where young people are unemployed for more than six
months and the long-term unemployed are concentrated.

This casts a different light on the welfare to work
programme. Do not think of it as a national programme.
There are 330 travel to work areas (effectively catchment
areas for welfare to work), although of very different sizes.
Some 25 per cent of the young people eligible for the New

Deal are concentrated in just three of these: London, Birmingham and Liverpool. Over 50 per cent of the long-term unemployed eligible for the New Deal come from just 18 areas. Over one-third of the New Deal budget will therefore be going to just six cities – London, Birmingham, Liverpool, Glasgow, Manchester and Newcastle. These are completely different parts of the country from the areas where unemployment is low and job vacancies are to be found. There are many parts of the country where employers will be hard-pressed to find more than a couple of dozen young people who have been unemployed for more than six months. The areas of high unemployment have few vacancies and may well have few employers able to participate in the scheme.

Is welfare to work the best single measure for dealing with social exclusion? Before we can answer that question we need to understand the problems that lie behind social exclusion.

The changing ghetto

Think of a traditional ghetto – the Jews in the cities of Central Europe or the American blacks in places like Harlem in the days of systematic discrimination. Perhaps the closest we have got in this country is Catholics in areas like West Belfast before the civil rights movement got under way. These are whole communities facing systematic discrimination from outside. They have their own businesses and leaders and their own schools and churches. Everyone is in it together. They are surrounded by a hostile world. The barriers then come down. The discrimination largely ends.

New opportunities open up and people are free to move. The ones who can, move out to the affluent suburbs which were previously barred to them. The places they leave behind are not classic ghettoes any more, they are inner cities and may well be far worse. America is the clearest example of this. It is the most mobile society and yet has some extraordinarily derelict and depressed areas. The good (mobility and opportunity) and the bad (depression and decay) are closely linked.

Welfare to work is now to be implemented in such depressed areas. Assume that everything which Ministers claim for the programme is valid and it does make some of these young people more employable. What do the young beneficiaries of the programme go and do?

We have already seen that there are not many job vacancies in these areas. The participants are not all going to be able to find themselves paid work in the commercial sector. They may therefore end up in the public sector or with the environmental task-force (exactly the criticism levelled at previous schemes). However, ministers have said that they hope welfare to work is going to help solve the nation's skills shortages, and we know where the job vacancies are. If participants move to these areas, welfare to work would become the 'on your bike' scheme for the late 1990s. It might help individuals who are socially excluded while doing nothing for the places which suffer social exclusion.

The Americans have an expression for it – spatial mismatch. William Julius Wilson in Chicago has studied at great length the problem of people who have become trapped in long-term unemployment because they have become detached from where the jobs are. The most forceful British advocate of this argument is again David Webster of Glasgow. In his recent Budget, Gordon Brown appeared to recognise this point by making £15 million available under the 'New Deal for Communities'. This represents less than 0.5 per cent of New Deal spending.

Seen from this perspective, welfare to work does little to bring jobs to the people but it might (if ministers' claims prove true) make it easier for some people to move to where the jobs are. It fails to deal with the structural problems which are holding back these areas, but becomes instead the labour market equivalent of the Assisted Places Scheme. That is to say, the New Deal may improve the life chances of certain individuals, but will do nothing to mitigate the original cause of their lack of opportunity in their home towns and cities.

8: What Could Be Done Instead

We have seen that the New Deal faces a series of pertinent criticisms. The most important of these is that a government committed to such tight control of public expenditure over so many areas is wasting the £3.5 billion it has raised from the windfall tax on a scheme as extravagant and as ill-thought-out as this one appears to be. The money could and should have been put to much better use.

What would a better programme look like? What follows is not, nor is it intended to be, party policy – which would have excluded the windfall tax in the first place. Instead it is simply an exercise to point to an alternative approach which this government could have taken. It has eight elements.

First, abolish age rules in the welfare to work scheme. There is no case either in natural justice or in terms of improving the prospects of the unemployed to spend so much on one narrow group and relatively less on everyone else. Any fair scheme should not discriminate on the grounds of age any more than it should discriminate on the grounds of race or creed. So have one programme aimed at giving extra help for all people who have been unemployed for more than one year. Instead, therefore, of focusing on 118,000 young people unemployed for more than six months and 216,000 people unemployed for more than two years the programme would be targeted on 398,000 people unemployed for more than one year.

Second, recognise that for many of these long-term unemployed the problem is that employers believe there is something wrong with them and some of the unemployed may even have come to share this fear. All the evidence from Britain and around the world is that the most effective way to help them is to overcome these barriers of distrust and doubt. You do not need an expensive six-month employer's subsidy to overcome these barriers. Instead you can build on the experiences of Job Clubs and Project Work to work intensively with these people to make them job-ready. It would not be a matter of bogus promises to offer them ambitious training opportunities. It would simply be making sure that they had a good CV, that they presented well in interview, and that they were motivated to get back into work. One could also extend the very successful Job Trial pilots which the previous government launched. Employers could take on a person who had been unemployed for more than a year with the state paying their wages for the first three weeks. After that it would be open to either party to end the arrangement. If employer and employee were both happy the placement would become a normal commercial job with no further subsidy.

Third, recognise that for those unemployed people who could not be made job-ready so easily, the basic problem is not training but education. We should not allow the pursuit of NVQs to get in the way of the overriding need for remedial education. The sad fact is that the welfare to work pilots have shown that up to 50 per cent of the unemployed people that they are dealing with have serious problems of literacy and numeracy. They need educational programmes focused very simply on the basics of reading, writing, and literacy. Employers are often happy to carry out their own training, and may well want to do so free from obligations to tie in with training requirements such as NVQs. But what they do want is to be able to recruit someone who can address an envelope, answer the telephone presentably, fill in a form and operate a keyboard. The intensive remedial education scheme would be aimed at dealing with those problems.

Fourth, one would need a backstop so that everybody who is unemployed for more than one year is definitely engaged actively in seeking work. If there were suspicions that someone had either given up or was working on the side, an effective way would need to be found of testing their commitment to work. Environmental improvement schemes could be used for this purpose. If someone turned down a place on one of these schemes that would be prima facia evidence that they were not actively seeking work. There would no obligation for everyone to participate in such a scheme. If a person who had been unemployed for more than a year was actively involved in job-search, perhaps getting help with special education and training and was doing their best, they would only go on to such an environmental task-force if they wanted to. But if there were doubts, the environmental work should be available as an option which could not in the last resort be refused without loss of benefit.

Fifth, the private sector could do more as a contractor to look after the long-term unemployed. They would be invited in some areas to take over the management of the entire caseload. Statutory rights to benefit would remain but if the private contractor could do better than the average performance so far in getting people off benefit and into work there would be a performance-related bonus for them. The Social Market Foundation has already published a pamphlet on 'America Works', describing such a scheme.

This five-part programme would cost far less than the New Deal and help rather more unemployed people. The savings would come from cutting back on ambitious training subsidies and on the six-month job subsidy to people who got into private employment. It is a much more robust, practical and realistic scheme. Any money saved out of the £3.5 billion budget could then be put into seriously addressing the problems of social exclusion. One could construct a misery index of rates of unemployment, family break-up, low school performance, and identify the 25–50 areas which suffered the worst. The significant savings from the universal welfare to work scheme could then be targeted particularly on these areas.

The sixth element of this alternative programme therefore would be to make all such areas enterprise zones, automatically using some of the money saved to compensate local authorities for the loss of the Business Rate. Planning controls would be relaxed. The minimum wage would certainly not apply. There could be other tax breaks for companies investing in these areas.

Next, one should recognise that for many unemployed people the best way back into work is through self-employment, an option largely ignored in the welfare to work scheme. The Enterprise Allowance scheme was very successful in helping people into self-employment, and one could finance an expanded Enterprise Allowance Scheme specifically for the target areas. This would enable people to carry on receiving benefit while they were in the early months of setting up self-employment or a small business.

Finally, any money left over could be put into a significant revamp of public-sector housing estates in these areas. But the extra money would be conditional on new partnerships with private landlords who would of course have to commit significant amounts of capital resource. As the enterprise zone regime would have weakened the planning controls there might be greater scope for development on brownfield sites of the sort which everybody is now keen to encourage.

How does this programme contrast with the government's welfare to work scheme? It spends less money on a select group of the unemployed. It recognises that job subsidies are a particularly expensive and ineffective way of helping unemployed people. It abandons any pretence at training. It instead tries to break down the two practical barriers which we know stand in the way of unemployed people getting back into work: their own and employers' doubts about their own job readiness; and basic literacy and numeracy. That would be the best way of ensuring the programme is effective and well targeted.

Then any savings could be used to do more to help with the structural problems in our most deprived areas. These are measures that would offer the genuine hope of economic revival rather than merely paying so much to a small number of individuals that they might be able to flee from the unpromising circumstances to which their less favoured contemporaries remain condemned. This is not an official programme, it is simply intended to show what would be an alternative and more effective model of job creation than the programme now being implemented.

Papers in Print

SMF Papers

1. The Social Market Economy
   Robert Skidelsky
   £3.50

2. Responses to Robert Skidelsky on the Social Market Economy
   Sarah Benton, Kurt Biedenkopf, Frank Field, Danny Finkelstein, Francis Hawkings,
   Graham Mather
   £3.50

3. Europe Without Currency Barriers
   Samuel Brittan, Michael Artis
   £5.00

4. Greening the White Paper: A Strategy for NHS Reform
   Gwyn Bevan, Marshall Marinker
   £5.00

5. Education and the Labour Market: An English Disaster
   Adrian Wooldridge
   £5.00

6. Crisis in Eastern Europe: Roots and Prospects
   Robin Okey
   £4.00

7. Fighting Fiscal Privilege: Towards a Fiscal Constitution
   Deepak Lal
   £4.00

8. Eastern Europe in Transition
   Clive Crook, Daniel Franklin
   £5.00

9. The Open Network and its Enemies:
   Towards a Contestable Telecommunications Market
   Danny Finkelstein, Craig Arnall
   £5.00

10. A Restatement of Economic Liberalism
    Samuel Brittan
    £5.00

11. Standards in Schools: Assessment, Accountability and the Purposes of Education
    John Marks
    £6.00

12. Deeper Share Ownership
    Matthew Gaved, Anthony Goodman
    £6.00

13. Fighting Leviathan: Building Social Markets that Work
    Howard Davies
    £6.00

14. The Age of Entitlement
    David Willetts
    £6.00

15. Schools and the State
    Evan Davis
    £6.00

16. Public Sector Pay: In Search of Sanity
    Ron Beadle
    £8.00

17. Beyond Next Steps: a Civil Service for the 1990s
    Sir Peter Kemp
    £8.00

18. Post-Communist Societies in Transition: A Social Market Perspective
    John Gray
    £8.00

19. Two Cheers for the Institutions
    Stanley Wright
    £10.00

20. Civic Conservatism
    David Willetts
    £10.00

21. The Undoing of Conservatism
    John Gray
    £10.00

34. Ready for Treatment
    Nick Bosanquet and Stephen Pollard
    £10.00

35. The Future of Welfare
    ed. Roderick Nye
    £10.00

36. Welfare to Work
    David Willetts
    £10.00

Reports

1. Environment, Economics and Development after the 'Earth Summit'
   Andrew Cooper
   £3.00

2. Another Great Depression? Historical Lessons for the 1990s
   Robert Skidelsky, Liam Halligan
   £5.00

3. Exiting the Underclass: Policy towards America's Urban Poor
   Andrew Cooper, Catherine Moylan
   £5.00

4. Britain's Borrowing Problem
   Bill Robinson
   £5.00

Occasional Papers

1. Deregulation
   David Willetts
   £3.00

2. 'There is No Such Thing as Society'
   Samuel Brittan
   £3.00

3. The Opportunities for Private Funding in the NHS
   David Willetts
   £3.00

4. A Social Market for Training
   Howard Davies
   £3.00

17. Stakeholder Society vs Enterprise Centre of Europe
    Robert Skidelsky, Will Hutton
    £10.00

18. Setting Enterprise Free
    Ian Lang
    £10.00

19. Community Values and the Market Economy
    John Kay
    £10.00

Other Papers

Local Government and the Social Market
George Jones
£3.00   .

Full Employment without Inflation
James Meade
£6.00

Memoranda

1. Provider Choice: 'Opting In' through the Private Finance Initiative
   Michael Fallon
   £5.00

2. The Importance of Resource Accounting
   Evan Davis
   £3.50

3. Why There is No Time to Teach:
   What is wrong with the National Curriculum 10 Level Scale
   John Marks
   £5.00

4. All Free Health Care Must be Effective
   Brendan Devlin, Gwyn Bevan
   £5.00

5. Recruiting to the Little Platoons
   William Waldegrave
   £5.00

6. Labour and the Public Services
   John Willman
   £8.00

7. Organising Cost Effective Access to Justice
   Gwyn Bevan, Tony Holland and Michael Partington
   £5.00

8. A Memo to Modernisers
   Ron Beadle, Andrew Cooper, Evan Davis, Alex de Mont,
   Stephen Pollard, David Sainsbury, John Willman
   £8.00

9. Conservatives in Opposition: Republicans in the US
   Daniel Finkelstein
   £5.00

10. Housing Benefit: Incentives for Reform
    Greg Clark
    £8.00

11. The Market and Clause IV
    Stephen Pollard
    £5.00

12. Yeltsin's Choice: Background to the Chechnya Crisis
    Vladimir Mau
    £8.00

13. Teachers' Practices: A New Model for State Schools
    Tony Meredith
    £8.00

14. The Right to Earn: Learning to Live with Top People's Pay
    Ron Beadle
    £8.00

15. A Memo to Modernisers II
    John Abbott, Peter Boone, Tom Chandos, Evan Davis, Alex de Mont, Ian Pearson MP,
    Stephen Pollard, Katharine Raymond, John Spiers
    £8.00

16. Schools, Selection and the Left
    Stephen Pollard
    £8.00

17. The Future of Long-Term Care
Andrew Cooper, Roderick Nye
£8.00

18. Better Job Options for Disabled People: Re-employ and Beyond
Peter Thurnham
£8.00

19. Negative Equity and the Housing Market
Andrew Cooper, Roderick Nye
£6.00

20. Industrial Injuries Compensation: Incentives to Change
Dr Greg Clark, Iain Smedley
£8.00

21. Better Government by Design: Improving the Effectiveness of Public Purchasing
Katharine Raymond, Marc Shaw
£8.00

22. A Memo to Modernisers III
Evan Davis, John Kay, Alex de Mont, Stephen Pollard, Brian Pomeroy,
Katharine Raymond
£8.00

23. The Citizen's Charter Five Years On
Roderick Nye
£8.00

24. Standards of English and Maths in Primary Schools for 1995
John Marks
£10.00

25. Standards of Reading, Spelling and Maths for 7-year-olds in Primary Schools for 1995
John Marks
£10.00

26. An Expensive Lunch: The Political Economy of Britain's New Monetary Framework
Robert Chote
£10.00

27. A Memo to Martin Taylor
David Willetts
£10.00

Trident Trust/ SMF Contributions to Policy

Hard Data

3. Universal Nursery Education and Playgroups
   Andrew Cooper, Roderick Nye
   £5.00

4. Social Security Costs of the Social Chapter
   Andrew Cooper, Marc Shaw
   £5.00

5. What Price a Life?
   Andrew Cooper, Roderick Nye
   £5.00

Centre for
Post-Collectivist Studies

1. Russia's Stormy Path to Reform
   Robert Skidelsky (ed.)   .
   £20.00

2. Macroeconomic Stabilisation in Russia: Lessons of Reforms, 1992–1995
   Robert Skidelsky, Liam Halligan
   £10.00

3. The End of Order
   Francis Fukuyama
   £9.50

Briefings

1. A Guide to Russia's Parliamentary Elections
   Liam Halligan, Boris Mozdoukhov
   £10.00